THE WOOLLY MONKEY MYSTERIES

THE **QUEST** TO **SAVE** A **RAIN FOREST** SPECIES

SANDRA MARKLE

Millbrook Press • Minneapolis

For Joanne Sprunger and all the young readers at Wea Ridge Elementary School in Lafayette, Indiana

For more digital content, download a QR code reader app on your tablet or other smart device. Then scan the QR codes throughout the book to see and hear woolly monkeys in their natural habitat.

The author would like to thank the following people for sharing their enthusiasm and expertise: from the CREES Foundation team—Ruthmery Pillco Huarcaya (researcher, Universidad Nacional de San Antonio Abad del Cusco, Peru), Dr. Andrew Whitworth (researcher, University of Glasgow, Scotland), and Quinn Meyer (founder, CREES Foundation, Peru); Kate McCrae, a.k.a. Wildlife Kate, UK Bushnell ambassador; Dr. Pablo Stevenson, Universidad de Los Andes, Colombia; Dr. Sam Shanee, founder of Neotropical Primate Conservation, Peru.

A special thank-you to Skip Jeffery for his loving support during the creative process

Millbrook Press
A division of Lerner Publishing Group, Inc.
241 First Avenue North
Minneapolis, MN 55401 USA

For reading levels and more information, look up this title at www.lernerbooks.com.

Main body text set in Futura Std Medium 13/18. Typeface provided by Adobe Systems.

Library of Congress Cataloging-in-Publication Data

Names: Markle, Sandra, author.
Title: The woolly monkey mysteries : the quest to save a rain forest species / by Sandra Markle.
Description: Minneapolis : Millbrook Press, [2019] | Series: Sandra Markle's science discoveries |
    Audience: Age 8–12. | Audience: Grade 4 to 6. | Includes bibliographical references and index.
Identifiers: LCCN 2018022839 (print) | LCCN 2018026921 (ebook) | ISBN 9781541543898 (eb pdf) |
    ISBN 9781512458688 (lb : alk. paper)
Subjects: LCSH: Woolly monkeys—Juvenile literature. | Endangered species—Conservation—Juvenile
    literature.
Classification: LCC QL737.P915 (ebook) | LCC QL737.P915 M37 2019 (print) | DDC 599.8/58—dc23

LC record available at https://lccn.loc.gov/2018022839

Manufactured in the United States of America
1 - 43014 - 27693 - 9/12/2018

CONTENTS

Ruthmery Pillco Huarcaya is a scientist from Universidad Nacional San Antonio Abad del Cusco, Cusco, Peru, studying woolly monkey behavior.

SCIENCE STAKEOUT

IN THE LEAFY RAIN FOREST CANOPY, HIGH OVERHEAD, MORE THAN A DOZEN WOOLLY MONKEYS ARE SPREAD OUT ALONG THE BRANCHES. Nearly 100 feet (30 m) below on the forest floor, Ruthmery Pillco Huarcaya watches them intently through her binoculars.

Although she doesn't want to miss anything, Ruthmery lowers the binoculars to wipe the sweat from her eyes. It's only six o'clock in the morning, and the air is already steamy. It's always hot in this part of the rain forest in Peru's Manú Biosphere Reserve, a protected conservation area next to Manú National Park.

This aerial view shows Manú National Park. Along with Manú Biosphere Reserve, the area is home to animals and plants found nowhere else on Earth.

5

Manú National Park, where Ruthmery is conducting her research, is one of the largest parks in South America, covering 5,918 square miles (15,328 sq. km). The Manú Biosphere Reserve covers another 992 square miles (2,570 sq. km). Alongside them is the Manú Cultural Zone, where people live but the land and wildlife are still protected. Together, these conservation areas cover a large area of land, but there's more to the park than the area it covers on the ground.

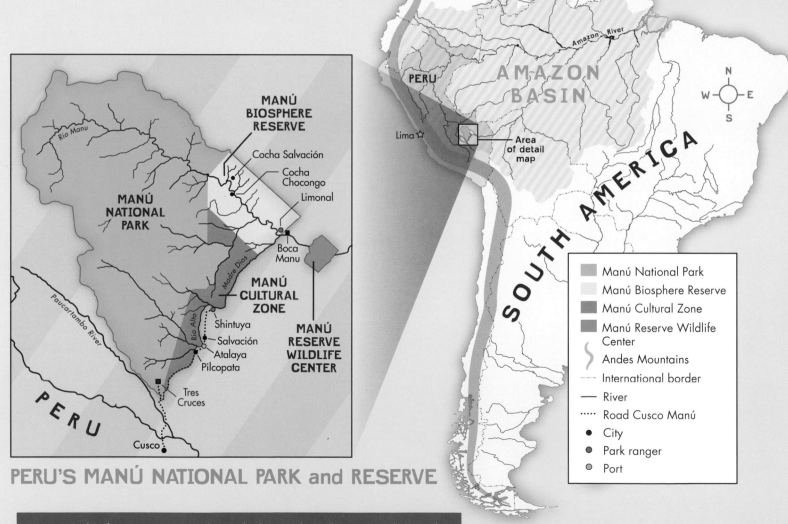

PERU'S MANÚ NATIONAL PARK and RESERVE

MANÚ BIOSPHERE RESERVE

Cocha Salvación

Cocha Chocongo

Limonal

MANÚ NATIONAL PARK

Rio Manu

Boca Manu

MANÚ CULTURAL ZONE

MANÚ RESERVE WILDLIFE CENTER

Madre Dios

Paucartambo River

Rio Alto

Shintuya

Salvación

Atalaya

Pilcopata

Tres Cruces

Cusco

PERU

AMAZON BASIN

Amazon River

PERU

Lima

Area of detail map

SOUTH AMERICA

N
W E
S

- Manú National Park
- Manú Biosphere Reserve
- Manú Cultural Zone
- Manú Reserve Wildlife Center
- Andes Mountains
- International border
- River
- Road Cusco Manú
- City
- Park ranger
- Port

A network of rivers running through the park and reserve drains the high mountains. These rivers are key to keeping the forest healthy.

Woolly monkeys live in groups that average around twenty adults and young adults, though a large group may include as many as forty monkeys.

Manú National Park is a sprawling lowland rain forest in the Amazon basin that climbs the eastern side of the Andes Mountains. There, up as high as nearly 13,000 feet (3,962 m) above sea level, the rain forest becomes cloud forest. The cloud forest is an extraordinary part of the world because, while it receives a lot of rainfall, the mountain elevation causes the air to be cool. This means the tree canopy is constantly swallowed up in clouds, while close to the ground, the air is full of misty fog. This unique environment is home to plants and animals found nowhere else on Earth. This combination of rain forest and cloud forest is home to the woolly monkeys Ruthmery is studying.

Since these monkeys spend nearly all of their time high up in treetops, their lives have been largely a mystery. However, thanks to determined scientists such as Ruthmery and some new technology, the mysteries are being solved. The woolly monkey's secrets can finally be revealed.

RAIN FOREST GARDENERS

A woolly monkey's long tail helps it stay balanced as it leaps and also helps it grab hold when it lands.

WHY IS IT IMPORTANT THAT SCIENTISTS SOLVE MYSTERIES ABOUT HOW WOOLLY MONKEYS LIVE AND WHAT THEY NEED TO THRIVE? It's because woolly monkeys are the rain forest's gardeners. These monkeys travel through the rain forest canopy eating fruit from trees. A woolly monkey's digestive system can't break down the seeds in fruit pulp, so the seeds end up in their waste. If the waste lands on soil, the seeds may sprout.

The heavier a monkey is, the more energy it uses traveling through the trees. To remain as light as possible, woolly monkeys need to pass waste often.

This woolly monkey's waste is filled with fruit seeds. Scientists study waste such as this to learn more about what these monkeys eat.

Over time, these dropped seeds grow into young trees that eventually replace the old trees that die and fall to the forest floor. The monkeys' waste that traveled with the seeds also helps fertilize the tiny new tree.

Each woolly monkey group cycles through a home range of about 400 acres (162 ha) during the rain forest's rainy season and as much as 1,900 acres (769 ha) during the dry season. As long as the woolly monkey population stays healthy and continues its gardening—by dropping seeds—the rain forest will keep growing and regrowing.

The woolly monkeys are key to ensuring the rain forest continues to be home to the unique tree varieties growing there. Those trees are necessary to support all the different kinds of animals living there. In fact, woolly monkeys are so important to the rain forest ecosystem that they're considered a keystone species. This means the rain forest wouldn't be the same without them. Learning more about this monkey isn't important just because scientists like Ruthmery are curious—it's critical to the survival of the rain forest.

emergent layer

canopy

understory

forest floor

RAIN FOREST FROM THE TOP DOWN

Tropical rain forests cover only about 6 percent of Earth's surface, and only about 2.5 percent of those are mist-filled cloud forests. Together, these rain forests are home to more than half of all the world's different kinds of plants and animals—many found in no other ecosystem on Earth. Explore the layers of a neotropical rain forest, meaning a rain forest located in Central or South America, and discover where woolly monkeys spend most of their time.

Emergent Layer (Up to 250 Feet/76 M, Aboveground)

This layer is made up of the very tallest trees poking out of the top of the rain forest. These giants usually also have big trunks. They have to be big to withstand the full blast of winds, rainstorms, and the sun's heat. This layer is home to animals such as harpy eagles, hummingbirds, spider monkeys, bats, snakes, butterflies, and insects. **Woolly monkeys visit here.**

Canopy (Up to about 150 Feet/45 M Aboveground)

The canopy is a dense layer made up of most of the forest's treetops. Here, rain filters down through the leaves as a mist, sunlight is less intense, and there is little air movement. There are always some trees in bloom and fruiting. Animals such as toucans, squirrel monkeys, sloths, tree frogs, snakes, and many kinds of insects make their home in this layer. **Woolly monkeys spend most of their time here.**

Understory (from the Bottom of the Canopy to the Forest Floor)

Young trees, shorter trees, and shrubs are in this layer. The light is dimmer as it filters through from above. It is home to lots of insects, including bees, bullet ants, stick insects, butterflies, and mosquitoes. There are also spiders, geckos, snakes, lizards, tree frogs, salamanders, bats, and jaguars. **Woolly monkeys sometimes visit here.**

Forest Floor (Ground Level)

Here it's very shadowy and dim. The air is also humid and still. The ground may be flat or mountainous. Fallen branches and trees drop here and, over time, rot. Plant matter and animal remains quickly decay here and, with the help of tiny living things, become part of the soil. It's home to animals such as scorpions, beetles, army ants, termites, peccaries, giant anteaters, jaguars, ocelots, and pumas. **Woolly monkeys very rarely visit here, but the seeds they drop in their waste lands here. Those that sprout grow into new trees.**

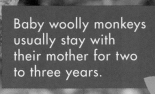
Baby woolly monkeys usually stay with their mother for two to three years.

MYSTERIES OF THE WOOLLY MONKEY

A NUMBER OF SCIENTISTS IN DIFFERENT AREAS HAVE BEEN STUDYING WOOLLY MONKEY POPULATIONS. Together, their discoveries have helped to provide pieces of a more detailed picture of the lives of these fascinating creatures. Studying woolly monkey waste revealed that while these monkeys sometimes eat leaves, insects, frogs, and even small birds, they mainly eat fruit—a lot of fruit. Pablo Stevenson, whose research for the Universidad de los Andes in Bogotá, Colombia, has included studying the behavior of woolly monkeys since 1988, noted, "In some areas, on average, woolly monkeys pass wastes as much as fifteen times a day." That means a lot of fruit seeds are dropped as groups of monkeys travel through their home range.

WOOLLY MONKEYS AREN'T ALL ALIKE

Woolly monkeys are among the largest monkeys in the rain forests of South America. Some live in lowland rain forest areas. Others live in high cloud forests. All woolly monkeys are similar in that they have bodies covered with short, thick fur—perfect protection against the sun, rain, and insect bites. Adults weigh about 17 pounds (7.7 kg) and have bodies about 19 inches (48 cm) long plus a long, fat prehensile tail that can wrap around something and hold on. Adults usually start reproducing when they're about seven years old. Babies develop for about seven to seven and a half months, and mothers usually give birth to only a single baby at a time.

Yellow-tailed woolly monkey

Lowland woolly monkey

Besides all the ways they're similar, some groups of woolly monkeys have different fur color and a somewhat different body size. In fact, for many years, scientists listed five different species of woolly monkeys. However, as Pablo Stevenson noted, "Recent DNA tests confirm there are only two species: yellow-tailed woolly monkeys and lowland woolly monkeys." Yellow-tailed woolly monkeys live only in the cloud forests of Peru. Lowland woolly monkeys are found in the rain forest areas of Bolivia, Brazil, Colombia, Ecuador, and Peru.

Scientist Sam Shanee (*left*) and his assistant, Fernando Guerra Vasquez, follow one of the approximately seven groups of yellow-tailed woolly monkeys in the area Shanee is studying.

Until Sam Shanee, founder of Neotropical Primate Conservation, arrived in the cloud forest of Peru, no one had studied yellow-tailed woolly monkeys there in about twenty years. Sam had been told there were fewer than 250 yellow-tailed woolly monkeys left in the wild. He's convinced there are really a few thousand, noting, "That still makes them critically endangered." He believes the reason for the low estimate was because observations from the ground had revealed so little about these monkeys.

Sam has been watching these monkeys for nearly ten years and stated, "Everything [I've discovered] about yellow-tailed woolly monkeys has been a surprise." In fact, he was shocked at how differently yellow-tailed woolly monkeys react to people being in their forest. Sam said, "Most monkeys run away from loud noises and people. But I saw yellow-tailed monkeys stay to shout and throw sticks at loggers." He worries that because they defend their home range in this way, yellow-tailed woolly monkeys are an easy target for hunters.

Sam also discovered another unexpected behavior that he observed repeatedly. Unlike lowland woolly monkeys, yellow-tailed woolly monkeys regularly come all the way down to the forest floor to drink from streams. And they sometimes eat dirt. Sam said, "We don't know if they're eating earth to supplement the minerals in their diet or if this helps them get rid of parasites." Parasites live off other living things and can make them sick and kill them.

Yellow-tailed woolly monkeys eat a lot more leaves and insects than lowland woolly monkeys do.

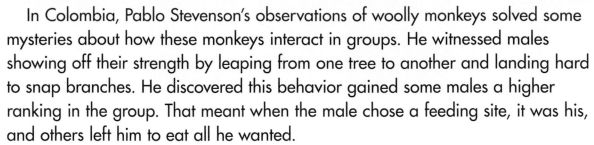

In Colombia, Pablo Stevenson's observations of woolly monkeys solved some mysteries about how these monkeys interact in groups. He witnessed males showing off their strength by leaping from one tree to another and landing hard to snap branches. He discovered this behavior gained some males a higher ranking in the group. That meant when the male chose a feeding site, it was his, and others left him to eat all he wanted.

Pablo's long hours observing woolly monkeys also gave him the chance to listen closely to these monkeys. He discovered individual monkeys make different sounds to communicate. They also repeat specific sounds during different behaviors. For example, the woolly monkeys he was tracking repeatedly made a kind of *pfew-pfew-pfew* whistle to keep track of one another.

Rather than attacking when they fight, males shout loud noises at one another.

Scan QR code to
view woolly monkeys
socializing in the rain
forest trees. Listen
carefully to pick out
their sounds from the other noises of
the rain forest. http://uqr.to/ci05

Like humans, each
individual monkey has
its own distinct voice.

Another time, Pablo saw a jaguar sneaking through the forest. He heard a woolly monkey bark: *Huh! Huh! Huh!* When the monkeys all took off through the treetops, he guessed this sound was a warning that this hunting cat was nearby.

He has also heard the woolly monkeys use a different warning for another kind of predator. "When a harpy eagle is nearby," he said, "I have heard the woolly monkeys make a very short, high-pitched whistle."

Continuing to observe woolly monkey groups from the forest floor, Pablo seeks to discover even more about how these monkeys interact and communicate with one another and how they work together to survive.

Woolly monkeys use their prehensile tail to stay safe in the treetops.

Since woolly monkeys move through the trees dropping waste and seeds as they go, they're key to replanting the forest. Scientists wanted to learn if the monkeys travel definite routes over and over through the forest, as if they were treetop highways. If they do, then scientists could work to help protect those trees from being cut down for wood or to clear the way for people to build roads or farms.

Camera traps give a chance for scientists to see what woolly monkeys do high in the rain forest canopy.

Of course, it's impossible for scientists to conduct rain forest stakeouts around the clock—or at all during some parts of the rainy season. And woolly monkeys spend nearly all of their time more than 100 feet (30 m) above the ground in the forest canopy. That makes them difficult to watch even with high-powered binoculars. Scientists needed an easier way to study woolly monkeys in the treetops. Luckily, they found one—the camera trap.

CAMERA TRAP IT!

A camera trap is a camera set up so an animal's movement triggers the photo. In the late 1890s, George Shiras III, a lawyer who was interested in photography and wildlife, invented the first camera trap. He set up a trip wire so that when an animal pushed or pulled on it, it triggered a magnesium flash powder unit to go off at the same time the camera took a picture. Called the father of wildlife photography, Shiras was dedicated to the protection of wildlife. He photographed animals in Michigan around Lake Superior to inspire others to protect land for wildlife. In fact, he worked on projects that led to the creation of parks and refuges for animals. Later, in the 1920s, Frank Chapman, a scientist studying birds, became the first to use camera traps to study animal behavior when he set camera traps on Barro Colorado Island in Panama.

This is one of George Shiras's first camera trap photos. The raccoon tugged on bait attached to the trip wire, triggering the camera and the bright flash.

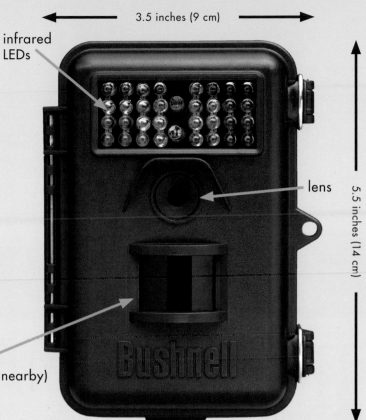

3.5 inches (9 cm)

infrared LEDs

lens

5.5 inches (14 cm)

The Bushnell Trophy Cam uses what's called a black flash trigger, meaning it uses an infrared light beam that neither humans nor animals can detect. Any animal breaking that beam causes the camera to take its picture.

passive infrared sensor (detects when an animal is nearby)

Early camera trap cameras were difficult to use. They were big and heavy at about 60 pounds (27 kg). They also needed a car battery for power and film, which had to be changed often. And the cameras weren't very weather resistant.

Camera traps have changed a great deal since the early models. Modern camera trap cameras are small, lightweight, and run on AA lithium batteries. The 119436 Bushnell Trophy Cam used to study woolly monkeys is only about 3.5 inches (9 cm) wide by 5.5 inches (14 cm) long—not much bigger than a standard cell phone. Without batteries, it weighs about 7 ounces (200 g)—slightly less than two sticks of butter. And, although it's twice as heavy when equipped with batteries, it is still lightweight. This camera can run for up to a year on eight batteries, take full-color high-density (HD) photos or record short videos, and save it all on a card that needs to be collected and replaced only every five to six months.

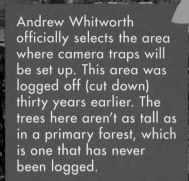

Andrew Whitworth officially selects the area where camera traps will be set up. This area was logged off (cut down) thirty years earlier. The trees here aren't as tall as in a primary forest, which is one that has never been logged.

TREE TOP MANÚ PROJECT

IN 2012, ANDREW WHITWORTH LAUNCHED A PROJECT TO STUDY WOOLLY MONKEYS WITH CAMERA TRAPS AS PART OF HIS GRADUATE STUDIES AT THE UNIVERSITY OF GLASGOW IN GLASGOW, SCOTLAND. The project, known as the Tree Top Manú Project, was supported by Conservation, Research & Education towards Environmental Sustainability (CREES). CREES is a Peruvian nonprofit organization that works to reduce poverty and protect the variety of animals and plants sharing the Manú Biosphere Reserve. Over time, Andrew trained a crew of graduate student assistants to help place and monitor the camera traps recording the woolly monkeys and other treetop animals.

Studying woolly monkeys with camera traps makes observing them easier than trying to watch them from the ground, but the cameras have to be placed high up in the rain forest trees. Andrew explained, "You don't just install a camera trap in any tree. You have to choose the right tree." That tree has to be one where woolly monkeys have been observed feeding or traveling along its branches. It also has to have a strong horizontal branch at least as thick as an adult man's thigh so it can anchor the climbing rope and support the climber who will place the trap.

Once a tree is chosen, a giant catapult hurls a weight attached to a thin line over the target tree branch. "That sounds easy, but shooting the weighted line high up into a tree without tangling it in vines or missing the target branch is tough," Andrew said.

Next, the thin line is used to pull two thick, heavy climbing ropes over the target tree branch. After that comes an anchor system: one end attaches to the tree, and the other end is what the person climbs. That's when the job becomes a real adventure—and really dangerous. It's time to head up to the top of the tree and attach the camera trap.

When Andrew and his team started to install the camera traps, their work was slow. Just getting the climbing line over the chosen branch could take hours.

Climbing into the canopy gave Andrew new insights into what living in the rain forest is like for woolly monkeys.

Bees, wasps, and bullet ants have attacked Andrew while he was suspended high above the ground. It's also hotter higher up in the forest canopy—up to 95°F (35°C)—and it's common to have sudden rain and wind gusts that make the tree sway. Andrew has endured suspension shock while climbing, the result of sitting for a long time in a harness with legs dangling, which slows blood flow to the legs.

Top: Andrew sometimes spends as long as two hours climbing to the canopy site where he'll attach the camera trap. He reported, "The highest I've ever climbed to install a camera trap is 147 feet [50 m]—about as high as a fourteen-story building."
Bottom: Bullet ants are just one of the insects found in the trees. Their sting is reported to hurt as much as being shot with a gun.

Andrew wears a climbing harness and an equipment bag that holds the camera and the supplies for attaching it to the tree. Anything forgotten would be a long way down on the ground.

Once at the chosen height, the climber often has to do what Andrew calls gardening, meaning clipping away vines or small branches that could block the camera. Next, the camera is strapped to the tree and programmed to either take just photos or both photos and videos. Finally, the camera's position is adjusted to aim the lens at the spot in the canopy the team wants to photograph and observe.

The results from the first camera trap test in 2012 were amazing enough to gain the project funding for more canopy-level camera traps. Andrew said, "In 2013, the Tree Top Manú Project added nine more camera traps for a total of eighteen recording woolly monkey behavior. In 2014, still more camera traps were added, bringing the total to thirty."

Ruthmery climbs a tree to place and check camera traps in the Manú Biosphere Reserve.

Because Ruthmery Pillco Huarcaya had been studying woolly monkeys from the forest floor, Andrew invited her to join the Tree Top Manú Project. Ruthmery accepted eagerly, even though it meant she had to learn to climb trees. She recalled, "I worked with a climbing trainer, but being high in the trees was scary at first. Then it was exciting to be so high up."

This is sapote (*Quararibea cordata*) fruit—one food that woolly monkeys eat often.

The camera trap photos gave Ruthmery new insights into woolly monkey behavior. For example, she learned that they continue to eat at night until seven o'clock or even later. She hadn't known this before because she had needed to stop watching them before that to be back in camp by dark.

Notice how the mother's prehensile tail helps her hold on while she rests and how the baby's tail is its safety belt.

See the challenges Ruthmery faces when observing woolly monkeys from the forest floor.
http://uqr.to/ci06

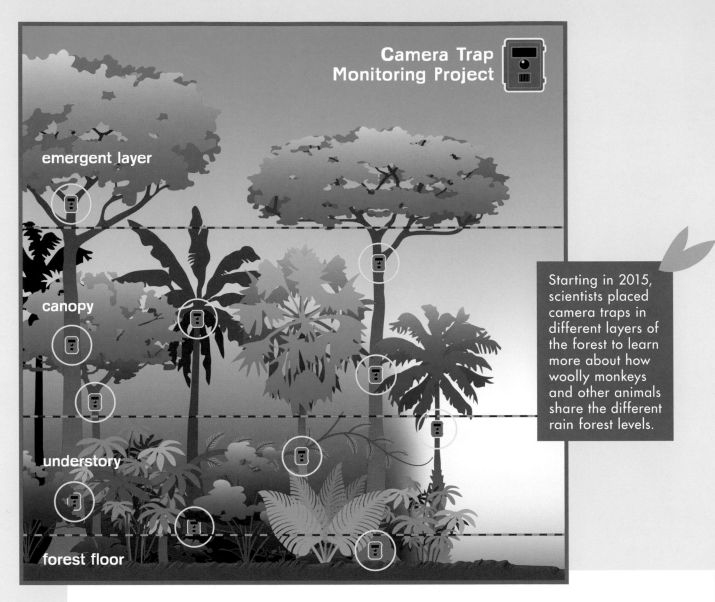

Camera Trap Monitoring Project

emergent layer

canopy

understory

forest floor

Starting in 2015, scientists placed camera traps in different layers of the forest to learn more about how woolly monkeys and other animals share the different rain forest levels.

After the Tree Top Manú Project's early findings were published in 2014, the project gained additional support from National Geographic Society and the Charles Darwin Foundation, and the team was able to add even more camera traps. By 2016, the project had 131 camera traps—88 high in the rain forest canopy and others at various lower levels. The Tree Top Manú Project had become the largest rain forest canopy camera trap monitoring project in the world.

With camera traps at different forest levels providing a peek into their world, scientists gained even more insights into woolly monkey behavior. For example, though these monkeys live in the upper canopy, they regularly climb up and down the trees—even going as low as the forest understory. The camera traps also captured photos and videos of animals no one knew were in that part of the Manú, such as a harpy eagle, a silky pygmy anteater, and a saki monkey.

Analyzing images from the camera traps increased the scientists' understanding that some trees in the rain forest are more important than others. There really are major pathways through the trees, enabling woolly monkeys—and other rain forest animals—to travel through the forest. As the woolly monkeys travel between feeding sites, they are dropping their waste, which is loaded with seeds. So along these pathways, seeds fall to the rain forest floor, sprout, and grow into future forest giants. Cutting down the trees that form those major pathways not only destroys large, full-grown trees, but it also removes the next generation of trees.

A camera trap caught these capuchin monkeys following one of the canopy highways.

This camera trap photo of a harpy eagle was a happy surprise. These birds are typically spotted only in primary forests, but this photo was taken in regrowth forest.

SOLVING NEW MYSTERIES

AS IS SO OFTEN THE CASE IN SCIENCE, DISCOVERING NEW INFORMATION LEADS TO MORE QUESTIONS. So it's no surprise that the more answers are found about woolly monkeys, the more new mysteries scientists find to solve.

Climate change is shifting weather patterns across Earth. Sam Shanee wonders what these changes could mean for the cloud forest and for the yellow-tailed woolly monkeys he studies. He said, "I'm worried about the effect of climate change on food availability, particularly during dry seasons." Food shortages might mean fewer monkeys are able to survive until the rain returns.

This baby yellow-tailed woolly monkey will soon begin to learn what fruit and leaves to eat by mimicking its mother.

What Ruthmery Pillco Huarcaya learned about the forest highways that woolly monkey groups travel along and the importance of key trees as bridges led to new questions too. She wonders how the woolly monkeys will deal with rain forest fragmentation (areas of rain forest cut off from the rest by logged-off areas). She wants to set up camera traps to see if woolly monkeys change their diet if they're forced to live in a forest fragment. She also wants to find out if woolly monkeys will come down from the treetops in such situations and cross open areas to reach other parts of the forest.

These yellow-tailed woolly monkeys watch tourists watching them.

INTO THE FUTURE

OF COURSE, IF RAIN FORESTS ARE TO HAVE A FUTURE, SOLVING MYSTERIES ABOUT WHAT'S NEEDED FOR THEM TO THRIVE ISN'T ENOUGH. Even governments setting aside areas as protected nature reserves isn't enough. Programs have to be put in place to help people understand why it's worth it to protect rain forests.

That's why the Manú Learning Center is presenting programs at local schools near the Manú Biosphere Reserve. These programs share information about the interconnectedness of the rain forest trees and the animals living there—a bond so strong one can't exist without the other. Along with CREES, the Manú Learning Center provides workshops that direct community efforts to replant and rehabilitate previously cleared rain forest areas.

With support from corporate partners, Conservation International supports a program aimed at stopping future deforestation, or clear-cutting large areas of forest. Through this program, any local farming family that commits to not cutting down rain forest trees to clear more land receives free training and help to improve crop yield on their current farmland.

Ecotourism is also helping. This trend of traveling to natural environments to see rare wildlife is bringing visitors—and money—to communities near the protected rain forest areas by attracting tourists from around the world. This provides yet another incentive for people to maintain the rain forest's health by protecting both the animals and the trees of the forest—that interconnected web of life.

In the past, female lowland woolly monkeys in the Manú were prime hunting targets because the babies were then sold as pets—a double loss to the rain forest.

CREES staff on the forest floor in the Manú Biosphere Reserve examine rain forest butterflies.

Thanks to scientists solving mysteries about the lives of woolly monkeys, people now know these monkeys play a key role in the future of the rain forests where they live. In fact, without woolly monkeys, the rain forests of Central and South America simply won't be the same. And those rain forests have to exist exactly as they are to be home to many different kinds of plants and animals—some found nowhere else in the world. The key to the rain forests' future is to ensure woolly monkeys continue to thrive so they can keep on being the rain forest's gardeners.

AUTHOR'S NOTE

When I read about the Tree Top Manú Project putting a record number of camera traps high up in the Manú Biosphere Reserve in Peru, I wondered what sort of discoveries scientists might be making. That's when I tracked down Andrew Whitworth, who was leading the effort to install the canopy camera traps. I was extremely impressed with the sheer effort the installation required. But then I learned the key part of having camera traps in the canopy was that they were helping scientists solve mysteries about the lives of woolly monkeys—monkeys about which very little was known because they live most of their lives high up in the trees.

I wondered why woolly monkeys were so important. When I interviewed Pablo Stevenson, who has studied them in neotropical rain forests for almost thirty years, I learned the answer. Woolly monkeys are key seed dispersers (spreaders)—in other words, the rain forests' gardeners. Wow! What an important and intriguing concept. And then I learned the populations of these important monkeys are shrinking.

While people are trying to help logged-off areas recover, we can't plant a rain forest—or even keep one healthy. There's something about the specific mix of different kinds of trees growing where they grow and being renewed by seeds dropping and sprouting that takes woolly monkeys and other rain forest animals. The rain forest's health is tied to the woolly monkeys, who have to eat, travel through the rain forest canopy, and drop their seed-filled waste to continually replenish the plant life.

If you've ever wondered why scientists go to such efforts to investigate the mysterious lives of animals, this research story reveals the answer for one such animal. Sometimes, as in the neotropical rain forests, parts of the world just can't be the same without the animals that live there. Woolly monkeys need the rain forests in order to survive, but these rain forests need woolly monkeys just as much. I loved discovering and sharing this scientific detective story that's working to ensure rain forests continue to have woolly monkey gardeners.

BE A SCIENCE DETECTIVE

This activity is one Sam Shanee did to get ready to investigate yellow-tailed woolly monkey behavior in the cloud forests of Peru. You can try it where you live.

With an adult partner, visit a park or other area where there are trees and you're likely to see squirrels. Take along a pencil and a notebook. Once you spot a squirrel, watch it for five minutes or as long as you safely can. Pay close attention to the following things:

- What are all the ways it moves (walking, running, climbing, leaping, or something else)?
- If it stops, how long does it stay before moving on?
- If it eats something, what does it eat? How does it eat? Does it eat a lot or a little?
- If it meets another squirrel, how does it act?

Write down what you observe in your notebook. On at least two other days, visit the same area to watch and record squirrel activities but go at different times of the day.

Read over your notes. What have you discovered about squirrel behavior? What is one thing you'd like to investigate by continuing to watch squirrels in action? If there aren't many squirrels where you live, choose a different animal to observe.

SOURCE NOTES

12 Pablo Stevenson, telephone interview with author, May 23, 2017.

13 Stevenson.

14 Sam Shanee, telephone interview with author, May 24, 2017.

15 Shanee.

15 Shanee.

17 Stevenson, interview.

23 Andrew Whitworth, telephone interview with author, August 11, 2016.

23 Whitworth.

24 Whitworth.

25 Whitworth.

26 Ruthmery Pillco Huarcaya, telephone interview with author, August 19, 2016.

30 Shanee, interview.

GLOSSARY

camera trap: a camera that uses a motion sensor or a light beam as a trigger to snap a picture, capturing wild animals on film without people being present

cloud forest: a high mountain forest where the air is usually cool and humid and clouds often hang at treetop level

deforestation: clearing a large area of trees

DNA: deoxyribonucleic acid, a chemical carrying all genetic information. DNA is found in the nucleus of nearly all cells in plants and animals.

ecosystem: a community of plants and animals that interacts within a natural environment

endangered: at risk of extinction, meaning no more exist

keystone species: a plant or animal vital to an ecosystem to the degree that, without it, the ecosystem would change dramatically or even cease to exist

neotropical rain forest: a rain forest in Central or South America

parasite: an organism that lives in or on another organism and gets its nutrients directly from it

predator: an animal that hunts and eats other living things to survive

prehensile: able to grasp. A prehensile tail can hold onto objects.

rain forest: a hot, humid forest near the equator made up of tall, densely growing, broad-leaved evergreen trees in an area of high annual rainfall. A rain forest is also known as a tropical rain forest.

species: a group of similar living things able to mate and produce babies that are also able to reproduce when they grow up

FIND OUT MORE

"Canopy Camera Trapping: Heightening Our Knowledge of Arboreal Mammals"
https://methodsblog.wordpress.com/2016/06/30/canopy-camera-trapping/
Enjoy photos of animals living in the rain forest canopy, and view a short video about how camera traps work and are set up in the treetops.

CREES Foundation: "Revealed: The Secretive World of Rainforest Animals"
https://www.crees-manu.org/revealed-secretive-world-rainforest-animals/
View camera trap footage from Tree Top Manú Project, supported by Conservation, Research & Education towards Environmental Sustainability (CREES). The CREES Foundation is a Peruvian nonprofit organization that works to reduce poverty and protect biodiversity in the Amazon rain forest, specifically in the Manú Biosphere Reserve. To find out more, visit www.crees-manu.org.

Fundacion EcoMinga: "Our Guards Luis and Santiago Recalde Climb into the Trees with a Troop of Woolly Monkeys!"
https://ecomingafoundation.wordpress.com/2015/08/25/our-guard-luis-recalde-climbs -into-the-trees-with-a-troop-of-woollu-monkeys/
Watch a video of woolly monkeys at play in their treetop home. Listen to a baby woolly monkey calling to its mother.

University of Glasgow: "40M High Treetop Camera Traps Capture Rare Amazonian Rainforest Wildlife"
https://www.gla.ac.uk/news/archiveofnews/2016/february/headline_445854_en.html
See the amazing rain forest wildlife captured on camera traps from the forest floor to the high treetops.

Williams, Zella. *Howler Monkeys and Other Latin American Monkeys*. New York: PowerKids, 2010.
Check out photos and learn more about how the monkeys of Latin America—including woolly monkeys—are key to their ecosystems and to local economies.

Yellow-Tailed Woolly Monkey Conservation
http://www.neoprimate.org/index.php/en/projects-npc/yellow-tailed-woolly-monkey -conservation
Learn more about conservation efforts to help yellow-tailed woolly monkeys in Peru.

INDEX

PHOTO ACKNOWLEDGMENTS

Image credits: © Crees Foundation, pp. 1, 22, 23, 24 (all), 25, 29 (all), 34; © Katie Lin, pp. 4, 7, 19; © CHARLIE HAMILTON JAMES/National Geographic Stock, p. 5; Laura Westlund/Independent Picture Service, pp. 6; 10–11, 28; © Tim Laman/National Geographic Stock, p. 8; © Nick Gordon/Minden Pictures, p. 9 (left); © Shanee/NPC, pp. 9 (right), 14; © Pete Oxford/Minden Pictures, p. 12; © Kevin Schafer/Minden Pictures, pp. 13 (top), 31; © Andrew Walmsley/NPC, pp. 13 (bottom), 15, 36; © Mark Bowler/Minden Pictures, pp. 16, 18, 32; © Cyril Ruoso/Minden Pictures, p. 17; © George Shiras/National Geographic Stock, p. 20; Courtesy of Bushnell, p. 21; Dr Morley Read/Stockbyte/Getty Images, p. 24 (bottom); Courtesy Ruthmery Pillco Huarcaya, p. 26 (both); © Steve Winter/National Geographic Stock, p. 27; © Jurgen and Christine Sohns/Minden Pictures, p. 33.

Cover: Amazon-Images/Alamy Stock Photo (woolly monkey); Toniflap/Alamy Stock Photo (background leaves).